The Eye Beholding

Also by Irene Wilkie and published by Ginninderra Press
Love and Galactic Spiders
Extravagance

Irene Wilkie

The Eye Beholding

Acknowledgements

'Taylor Square' and 'The Disappearing': *The Red Room Company*, 2012

'Tropical': *Poems 2013*, Volume 2, Australian Poetry Ltd Members' Anthology

'As you Pass Me In the Hall': *Australian Poetry Journal*, Volume 4, Issue 1, 2014

'Undersong': *Poetry and Place* Anthology 2015, Close-Up Books (First written for a film T*he Kitchen Table Poets,* 2012)

'Storm Flood': *Wonder Book*, Kit Kelen 2014

'Touching Down': *fourW twenty-five, New Writing* 2014

'From the Rotunda': *Poetrix*, Issue 38, Western Women Writers, May 2012

'Standing in Mud at Lake Edge': *The Way to the Well*, Central Coast Poets Inc., 2014

'Husband's Refrain': *Off the Path*, Central Coast Poets Inc., 2010

'The Last Hare': *Flashing the Square*, 2014, Spineless Wonders

'Only Then': *Yellow Moon*, December 2005

'The Cicadas Are Late This Year': *fourW twenty-four,* New Writing, 2013

'Nanna': *Writers' Voice,* 2009

'The Eye Beholding': W.B. Yeats Poetry Prize Australia, 2016, website

The Eye Beholding
ISBN 978 1 76109 224 4
Copyright © Irene Wilkie 2021
Cover image:

First published 2021 by
GINNINDERRA PRESS
PO Box 3461 Port Adelaide 5015
www.ginninderrapress.com.au

Contents

Early	7
Small Memories	8
Taylor Square	10
New Notes	12
Dragon	14
Undersong	16
Gallop	17
Playing the Light	18
Grandfather	20
Morning	22
Beating Like Wings	23
Pantomime	25
Tropical	26
From the Rotunda	28
Storm Flood	30
Afterthought	31
Standing in Mud at Lake Edge	33
The cicadas are late this year,	35
Nanna	36
Husband's Refrain	37
Caravan on the Beach	39
Water Melt	42
Respect	44
Feline Fog	45
Sitting With Doves	46
Only Then	47
Breakfast Notes	49
The Last Hare	50
Spillway	51
Pebble	53

Lake of Myth	54
Touching Down	56
Incident at the Gallery	58
Keys	60
As You Pass Me in the Hall	61
Flat Sea	63
The Lookout	65
A Small Delight	67
The Eye Beholding	68

Early

Waking before the sun,
in the shy early light
of damp-hushed greys,
the land waits.

Slow colours rise,
white parrots call,
yellow crests half-visible
against the muted greens
of pittosporum,
new summer grass.

The mountain devil's bloom
deepens into red,
becomes the honey-eater's feast.

A heron
brushes gold on the mountain-face.

The sun
washes in chardonnay.

Small Memories

1.

A sparrow hit the wall   a huge cherry-bump
on its unconscious head   with love we laid it
in a shiny cake-tin softly lined with silk.
We hovered   hoped   in the morning it was gone.

2.

And we acquired lice under our shiny plaits
behind the ears   I still feel the pain   the sting
of kerosene applied with vigour   our mother
protesting *Not the three of you   again.*

3.

I stole from Mr Wong   as many as I could hold
in my small blue bag   sweet unblemished apples
without a worm inside and my father dragged me back
to apologise in shame.   Mr Wong forgave us both.

4.

The classroom fed a thirst for exotic worlds
offered the magic carpet zooming over unknown
snowy peaks on wafts of chalk and dust
the smell of ink   old orange peel   wet shoes.

5.

On a demolition site   a broken pipe leaked
a green-edged brook   enchanted   wild
among sharp-edged bricks we looked for ships
dreaming on far rivers we had heard about.

6.

His kiss was very damp   his grasp a clamp.
This twelve-year-old knew nothing   but later
he courted each of us   one by one   we fled
his hungry hands   we still remember him.

Taylor Square

was the crossroad of my existence –
trams to Bondi
> to town
> to school
among the Moreton Bay figs.

On the road, we crowded,
waiting in marked spaces,
traffic brushing past,
too close;
we listened for wheel-grind
on metal tracks,
electric crackle overhead.
Here motorbikes skidded,
the paper-man yelled,
neon ads sizzled
and the smell of fuel,
of beer and vomit outside the pub,
of delicatessen rabbit
mixed
drifting to the gaol, the courthouse,
both elegant
in honey-coloured sandstone.

Taylor Square
that busy, honking convergence
was where
my father waited for me
to return from my first date –
we were late and he was so
unamused.
Our excuse, the scarcity of trams,
was true, really, really
but my father fumed,
the air electric.
I blushed at what he thought we'd done.
We were so young.
I never saw that lad again.

Muttering, four paces behind,
I followed my father home.

New Notes

Who is this?
Who is this singing?
I recognise old notes
sculptured into new.

I do know you.
How could I forget?
You were always in my vision's sweep –
since childhood, you carolled next door,
the fence between us, your voice a chime.

When you were grown, you charmed me –
I thrilled to the crystal threads,
the music through the bloodwoods.
Our voices rose, skimmed blue haze,
winged through the upper, the lower air,
arced through silver-misted streams.

When you left, I was frozen –
even in the sunlight.

It is you, isn't it? Have you returned
to resurrect my illusions?
You are singing those words,
I am here, here,
clear as a ringing bell.
I hear their promise,
but they don't tell me how long
you will stay – or if you will.

Your voice interrupts night shadows,
seeps as tendrils under eaves,
through skylights, the garden door –
a cool infusion of eucalypt and honey.
My quiet house stretches, blinks its eyes,
pushes me out from the sterile shell.
I follow blind threads, shuffle through rain,
find you in chorus with currawongs.

You look up, catch me staring, uncertain
but you don't stop the melody.

You beckon, offer the dawn –
our voices soar and soar again.

Dragon

The track is passable   no mud   but damp.
We push through new green shoots   bright
against the muted bush   the breeze of beach

and there's no one here.

Tall as a man   a goanna claws   rushes
up a eucalypt   thumps through leaves
slumps its belly on a white-skinned branch
four legs dangling.

It stares down   heaves with breath
black ribbon tongue busy testing air –
reptilian brain   devil eye
plan cunning strategies.

We don't give it time –
slithering down the dunes
we head for the mid-tide surf.
The beach is deserted   and ours

but that dragon owns the bush.

The lore says it is fond of eggs
soft creatures hidden in undergrowth.
We trust it also relishes
the flavours of wild rabbit.

Despite our curiosity we decide
that we don't need to linger
to learn its dragon habits or
admire its steely strength.

We map a path   behind it   round it
creep along the forest edge
quell the hammer of our hearts
and take the long way back.

Undersong

If there is sky,
if there is summer,
if the sob through the pines has dulled
to a small wing's minor beat,
to a cricket's pulsing breath,
the day radiates the sibilance of eucalypt,
thin leaf edges turn to the sun.

And if rain veils the canopy,
weaves errant threads of timpani,
if sandstone drips staccato
and braided runnels lilt a rippled tone,
then the creek fattens,
sings soft arias.

We dare not move or speak,
hear undersongs we won't disturb,
believe we don't belong, think
all will vanish
like the puff of a fungus ball,
leaf shift, beetle click, seed split.

Shy ducklings rustle reeds,
our whispers peal like thunder.

We breathe too much.

Gallop

Air whips
skin twitches
muscle grips
thighs stretch
bones arch
the spine
flexing
a welter of heat.

The tongue shrieks
passion gallops
rhythm thunders
through leaping hearts.

I am
breathless as the beast I ride
joyful as his bellow
hot as blood.

Playing the Light

Around the towering blocks
in the downtown night,
pigeons glide,
reflect the flash of neon.
Green flickers into burgundy,
flocks dive and rise, hover and loop,
playing the light.

They must be calling, one to the other
but here, on the street, the sound is lost
to passing horns, bells, radio thump.

They weave a silent mime,
a patterned, primeval festival
in a city not my own.

This ancient dance
to a modern theme
happens nightly
and I have never noticed.

I am here because your air
of knowing me
attracts my spirit.
If it were not for you,
I would be gone,
back to my own metropolis
and its warmer days.

I stay and wait and watch.
Your voice is mine;
we talk like long-time friends –
you show no hint of subterfuge.

Here is promise –
it seems the right thing;
I will not walk away.
See how you stand with me
in the midst of strangers
looking to the sky.

On a night-shadowed pavement,
we delight in colours
winking on and off
in the gentle choreography
high above our heads
and agree that this is rare.

Because of you, this city
might become my own.
Here may be bliss, or tears,
waiting to be tried.

Grandfather

He walked with me on squeaky sand;
through his eyes I first knew the sea,
probed its embrace,
the clocked tides, the roped boats.

This is what he told me:

when he was a fisherman,
his nets snared giant wings,
dragged into silence a strangled bird –
the look of ocean, sleek cry of tide,
an albatross
below the foam.

He slashed the bonds,
grappled with the stabbing beak,
freed the captive,
wiped blood from his salt-encrusted hands –
watched the slap of wings cut the air.

The white-crossed bird
flared into life, grace on blue,
turning, wheeling,
raced alongside, dipped to the bait again.

Grandfather cursed,
wound in empty nets –
set the rudder for home.

This is the story he could not tell:

beard flying, cheeks rutted,
eyebrows a glut of salt,
he pushed out his dinghy
from Bloodwood Cove,
took the tiller in a rattling sea,
navigated Whirlpool Rocks
and drove through the maelstrom
blur of reef –
a sailor's escape
from the welfare nurse,
the slow confusion of pills.

He greeted whales, the curiosity in their eyes,
the black tail-slap, the suck and wash.

The engine sputtered in the sudden flood –
far from the cliffs, ocean claimed his craft.
Perhaps he swam awhile in the wake
of whale and wave and perhaps
he thought of me.

This is how it may have been, or not.
The sea was his life and the end of it.
He offered himself to the sigh of shells,
the flicker of fish in shallow tides,
barnacle, kelp, anemone,
the quiet, embracing,
timeless sea.

Morning

upright on a shelf
an empty wine bottle

echoes the smile
of the nymph on the label

quickens the step
of the fellow in the garden

dances light
about the woman in the kimono –

reflects

Beating Like Wings

This is the hour
this happening out of the
dark sleep-well swooning
your breath away you clutch
beg him to do something
surprised he does not guess
the effort not to fall into
the mouth of panic the
sweat the flurry of arms
the knots the grey-blue-hot-
red-waves the hard-clench beat.

He dials in disbelief the event
too quick the idea of necessity
beginning to burn and this is
the time when he must make
the moves you know what you
cannot stop you know nothing
will help what is done the matter
of you letting go too soon and
the talk the heat the morning
grows bright outside you hear
them coming want to tell them
Thank God you're here.

Your feet won't grip the floor
your tongue slips words leap
inside the head flutter flap zing
as if against the bars of a cage.
You see
his relief as the medics walk in calm
calm in command and then you grab
his hand return the worried kiss let
go let go focus breathe begin the task
the clouded mask the siren rolls with the
quickening count.

He follows
with his impossible names
for a daughter or son the decision
will come flying will be so right when
the tiny face is real and sweet new lungs
echo down the hall.

You will make a choice at
last all doubt erased you
will hold this child
this girl or boy you don't know yet.

You will understand all history
all mysteries all ancient rites
the fiercest love
as you stroke the downy head
and hear two voices
call this child by name.

Pantomime

At the top of the station steps
I take his hand on the way
to a pantomime in town.

Halfway down, he sees a train depart.
Too young to know more must come,
he sobs for the dream,
for the promise lost.
I dry his tears and whisper,
Listen.
Can you hear it? Can you hear?

The distant humming, rumbling approach,
the thunderous light
excite despite the fears.

He wonders at the carriage doors,
the tingling departure bells.

In a tent on a city roof,
a beanstalk drama
and a boy called Jack,
are no longer myth –
then he laughs –
there is yet another delight.

He tugs my hand
for the journey home.

Tropical

Brush turkeys rake the sand,
beach grass and cuttlebone.
I settle in my damp deckchair,
salt drops slide,
broad hat shades
my fluttering magazine.

New learners, new surfers,
the latest lovers sprint from
the panting sea; he piggybacks
the squealing girl; brown toes curl.
He dares a pat to her derriere,
kisses her upturned face;
she drops sand into his shorts.

They think this place is theirs.

I put down my magazine,
lower my brim, retire
behind dark glasses,
scan the beach for cuttlebone,
brush turkeys on the sand.

The lovers go, leave me to guard
their mound of goods
while they tease, dive, slide
like dolphins about each other.

I watch, remembering, count
bags, red and yellow towels,
and the birds
deep-grunt, flap along edges
of shade, avoid
what is melting in the sun,
inspect, pass over
the barren grass,
forever scrape for something better.

Above their *quirk, quirk, quirk,*
helicopter beat, surf bluster,
I hear the shrieks of the loving two
cascade along the beach.
Here they are, skins glistening.

He dries her short-cropped head,
she plants her feet as if riding waves until
he bends to span, measure with broad hands
her slender waist;
she holds her breath, he holds a towel while she,
hardly shy, removes wet clothes for dry.

Brush turkeys parade
their orange-yellow necks,
their red and naked heads,
inspect beach grass,
peck at cuttlebone,
scratch and scratch the sand.

From the Rotunda

The tide is in ebb, its sculpturing work
done for the hour,
the curves, the etches.

A small boat rests on its side,
flies drone
to the dried stink of fish.

Red markers flag the shallow channel;
pacified lace edges
ripple in sleep.

Shearwaters lie matted, defeated,
claws curled, beaks open,
stopped with sand.

But when the hoodlum tide
blathers in,
upturns empty shells,
flurries black weed,
eats stone,
it shouts at the gale
in the banksia blooms.

From the rotunda
power lines whip,
twist like eels
and the lights explode.

The captured boat drags
its keel over rocks
beyond the channel,
blunders to the bay

and the dark, dead seabirds follow.

Storm Flood

Down from the hills
to the rock-barred river
the flash flood rises up like a snake,
black fangs clotted with red-soil foam,
body armoured with spear-ends of trees,
strikes over the causeway
the swamp, the dam,
shouts through the paddock
the valley, the town,
drowns new barley, the chicken coop,
swallows the bodies of cattle and men –

spews them into the sea.

Afterthought

That busy hen-woman
came running after me
as I rose to depart.
Ah, I smiled,
she's coming
to say 'Goodnight'
but she fluffed her best feathers
and flapped at me
the last raffle ticket in her book.

She hadn't spoken to me all night,
her elevated table
higher-toned than mine.
From her lofty, beady view,
my dining fellows and I
were of no account
and impecunious,
her only acknowledgment
a distant baring of the beak.

I should have bought it
really, I should
but knew I could never win.
A thin excuse. Instead I said
I'd just broken out
in chickenpox
that very minute and thus
my present health was frail
as an egg on rock.
She cocked her bristling comb,
flexed her daggered toes,
fluttered her stony intent
at some other hapless bird.

Unobserved, I flew outside
to hide
in the friendly night.

Standing in Mud at Lake Edge

I think of creatures that live buried in the dark –
the lack of eyes in a sunless underworld;
touch must be their colour, their moon, their sustenance,
their succulent skins their kinaesthesia,
the thing they know but don't,
just as we feel a sixth sense we cannot define,
calling it merely time-taught memory.

For us, nothing is blank; we can't conceive of black
as blank, nor white as a blanched-empty space;
stare at black canvas long enough and we are
surprised to see it lives, moves and jumps with
imagination, with sound, the roundness of slip and slap,
of ripples tiptoeing about our feet,
the wind pining blind through the casuarinas;
we supply a video, play it privately
on the vacant screen, a show for one.

Standing here, feet in the mud,
I note how light scintillates on water surfaces
above the blackness and is not diminished,
how smoke-feathers in the back hills join
with a downy drift of cloud,
how a transparent snail clings to a bent reed
unafraid in its frailty.

The voices of black swans bugle down
from their V-formation flight
and the sky,
blue, blue, lapis lazuli blue,
offers an intensity I retrieve
to lighten dreams
of the blackest night.

The cicadas are late this year,

only two or three emerge,
ring their rolling cadence
in single file
as if they want it known
their aim
is the usual procreation thing
despite the trying climate,
the extraordinary sun.

They retreat to some dark cavity,
preserve their gauzy wings, emerge
to belly-drum their roundelay sense
of rise and fall,
their understanding of nuance
in the surging, metallic thrum
of greengrocers, brown bakers, black princes
yet to join them in cacophonic melody.

Clawed on a smooth-limbed eucalypt,
they will chant in numbers,
lustrous, clustered,
pissing down
a fine and dewy mist,
fooling me,
then, shrilly dying,
will vanish until next year.

Nanna

Through the final haze
drifts only love

familiar voices
firm or weeping

scented blossom
so soon dying

In the sleep of faded memory
she stirs to touch

calm hands   warm
deft comfort
for the cooling heart

She whispers to people
she once knew –
dreams again

Blue stillness creeps
amid the sound of bells

Husband's Refrain

This time every year,
every time,
it is the same.

This year, this time,
things aren't any different
and who would want it?

Every year, every time
you say to me, *It's spring;*
you take my hand
and my feet dance with yours
on a lawn of jonquils,
through gardens wakened
by warming light.

You tune me in
to thoughts of swallows
renewing nests;
you discover blossom-burst
in jaded winter canopy

and from my bones the cold is gone
in my lone dreams
when I see the shine of your hair,
the curve of your toes,
the golden sandals.

When I am too lost to notice
how fast the seasons change
from blacks and purples,
to reds and yellows,
from frost to heat
or to watch the cheeky winds
ripple pale, new grass,
you remind me,
even in your absence,

each time, each year,
every time.

Caravan on the Beach

For a week we walked the beach, taught our children
the serious wisdoms
pertaining to everything –

footprints in wet sand   how
these belonged to a fox, those, a pelican
and there, on gouged earth among dead leaves
where wild dogs in a frenzied pack
ambushed a joey-kangaroo, a confusion of blood
on matted fur – and the children clung to us.

At lake edge, we noted differences
between our city home and here –
the muddy squelch of feet,
the susurrus of reeds in shallows,
the silence of the shy wood duck,
the croon of the black swan.

Stumbling on a dead campsite we
explained how hungry people stalk and trap,
leave bones, webbed feet and feathers
at this grey-ashed fireplace –
and the children shivered.
Were they already aware of death?

That year, round-eared bush mice abounded, became
food in an endless chain – for the owl, the hawk, the rat,
the snake, the huge goanna down the beach.
Such a pestilence for us. Inside the van, the children
watched mice move behind plastic-lined walls,
small roving bumps they tried to catch.

They found one spinning round the sink
and laughing, loved this native Mickey Mouse,
so different, so adorable. I said nothing.

We discovered how night-wild pigs snouted pipis
from wet sand at the lake's sea edge.
We heard but never saw them though everyone
could tell their expertise in the shattered shells
dropped beside the troughs they left behind.
The children began to fear shadows.

We used fresh bait for fishing, demonstrated how
to thread live pipis on a hook, to cast to a thrashing sea
where tailor, needle-toothed, chopped and gorged on
silver whiting twisted into the air, in desperate escape.
We reeled in attacker and attacked, the tailor, the whiting;
we filled our bags with gasping heaps of tail and fin.

There was good eating that night; their dad trimmed the catch,
I scaled, floured, pan-fried in oil a hot, fishy feast with lemon.
But the children cried over severed heads, moist eyes blank.

Next day we searched the rocks, trapped three hairy crabs,
dropped them live, but humanely stupefied, into a steaming pot.
Our brood would not eat, refused the soft, white flesh.

'This has got to stop,' we said. 'You have to learn –
food must be gathered, must be killed that you may eat.'
Their tearful wails said everything.

Eels slithered up from the lake, over the foam-washed berm,
met rising surf, then wriggled to the sea like snakes. At real risk,
we netted one, black and fat – and the children screamed.

Gaslights floating on a board, we scooped up glow-eyed prawns
risen out of weed. Their prehistoric look justified their sacrifice,
and the pink, peeled, fresh taste. But our offspring saw them as pets.

We quaffed oysters chiselled off the rocks, ate sea-urchin eggs
scraped raw from robotic shells. At full moon, the children,
grown alarmingly thin, preferred baked beans in tomato sauce.

The lesson wasn't sinking in; instead they searched for the creatures
with Mickey Mouse ears. They found none, amid long grass, on
slipping dunes – and how could they keep such captives?

The week was over, the holiday done. Gaslights and reels repacked,
we buried bones, shells and, secretly, a swag of mouse unfortunates.
We started the car and waved farewell to our wildly natural paradise.
But was it?

At home, car parked on the smooth driveway,
offspring and other essential goods unpacked,
I wondered what the children had learned.
I wondered what we had found in ourselves.

I dared not risk an answer.

Water Melt

A blue lake hovers distantly
above a road
that hurtles
undeviating through sand
and spinifex.

We yearn to bathe away
our salty sweat
but on approach
the water melts in filaments
of blue

then reappears   a lake on stilts
absurd   a clown
who tantalises
beckons   promises relief
somewhere

a jest to send us soaring up
above the road –
this line on a plain
through mallee scrub   the sinuous tracks
of dry river beds.

Hey   is that a water bore
with a tank and bench –
hot water on tap?
The landmark shape seems grounded,
solid with hope.

Maybe someone has left
a newspaper, a message,
a greeting in the desert   yes.
We push the pedal to the floor.
We fly.

Respect

west of the desert
on dry iron rocks
a fresh wallaby head
black lashes curled
rests neatly
on severed velvet paws
placed as thanks
for the gift
of flesh
of spirit
of hunger appeased
beneath a brittle sky
deepest blue

Feline Fog

Jaws clamped   like my hands
on the wheel   this fog is a cat

her eyes the small blood moons
on road posts – crawling past

She is white   thin   sometimes not
here   or here   grins and winks

This cat   the boss   full of jest
slides   wraps curves I cannot see

When the fog breaks into stars
she won't tell me where she goes

Sitting With Doves

Though plum blossoms hum
a perfumed foretaste,
my father says
the demise of the tree
will foretell his own.

The bark is brittle,
the old trunk bent,
the wind harps
through petals
daring them to fall.

My father wills
the roots to hold
the flower, the fruit
the leaf, the branch
for as long as his heart beats.

He sits with doves
listening to the weather.

Only Then

Drop your luggage at the door,
shake off the traffic fumes,
escape to a wild place.

Walk the path
through bloodwoods
to a panoply of orchids
blooming in their ancient way,
imitating wasps,
wearing leopard spots,
pink lashes, purple throats,
the trappings of seduction.

Hear the click of beaks –
black cockatoos
shred casuarina cones,
litter the forest floor;
gentle voices scrape
wire conversation.

Breathe softly,
the wonga pigeon
nods unafraid,
the bandicoot digs,
the spider weaves
a golden trap –
death with apology.

Perfume, pain,
decay, rebirth,
echo Gondwana.

Let the downbeat rhythm
hum your blood,
lateral light
slipstream your skin.

In the palpitating air,
expect the pith of things
to shape you
and then –
come inside.

Breakfast Notes

Dawnlight weaves shadows
on the white wall;
along the sculptured cornice
a small black spider creeps.

I hear your hands clink china cups,
open a drawer.
I smell coffee, bacon, toast
and you call me from my bed.

I stand, watch a distant car
wind down the mountain road
in the sudden purple burst
of sunrise on misted blue.

You call again; I smooth unruly hair,
find the kimono in flowered silk,
hurry to the kitchen; there you are
in those new, blue-striped pyjamas.

Beside the marmalade, wattle sprays
grace the table; outside the door,
some bird rattles its raucous note
of delirious rhapsody.

The Last Hare

The hare's long ears stand and turn. Survival is his tutored game. Ginger-haired and the size of a poodle, he lopes silently out of the bushland reserve. Here, politically misplaced, he should not be growing fat on environmentally conserved and native grasses, should not be stealing sustenance from the mouths of wallabies, should not be seeking diversity in my rose garden. He watches me and listens. I let him have his rose. He knows I am no shooter or fox or dog. I know where he shelters under flat sandstone. He knows I know and would invite me there if I could fit. It's a secret between us. The other secret I know but will never tell him is that he is the last hare in this reserve. He has made friends with the wombat under my house, the possum in my roof, the echidna in my garden – and me.

He is content. My roses bloom each day. There are plenty for us both.

Spillway

We can't tell which way the river flows, the surface
still;
a wood duck floats like thought in the late afternoon,
like a dream
water weed, not trailing east or north or west or south,
hangs
in trembling indecision.

Then the water stirs before an icy breath of air.
I say,
'Is that way north, where the wind blows?'
He laughs.
'See those reeds along the bank? Could they be leaning
south?'
We walk 'south'.
(Who knows? I think it could be east.)

We don't know this river and the sun is deep in cloud –
the map in the car
too easy a way to solve a mystery.
We play a game
to prove what we guess is true as we stretch and tease,
conceding
that it matters not at all.

We search along the edges, find a twig that floats awhile
then sinks;
dead leaves think in circles; we follow the path, follow until
a slow spillway
laces our river over and down the sloping face.

Late winter light shivers through movement barely visible,
a cross-hatch
of near silence until I touch and flick fine drops across his lips
about to tell me,
'There. The river is flowing south – and that way is south.'

We watch the weaving spill below the path and out the other side,
hear not just another stream
flowing west to east or north to south
or any way else.

It's the murmur against the pebbled moss,
as an answer,
the cloud reflection at dusk
as a reason
for a certain filling of the heart.

Back in the car, we unfold the map,
let it define parameters.
Surprised, we learn
this river bend is flowing west.

Calmed, we drive slowly into town.

Pebble

This pebble, worn smooth,
a shape ground down
from angularity
through boisterous rolling
over and over
at the whim
of region, time and weather,
changed in the hot squeeze
of earth's grinding plates
far beneath sky's watch,
old as earth and older,
atoms rearranged,
has travelled
mute,
unresisting
to rest in my impermanent hand.

Lake of Myth

On a lake edge in Scotland,
ripples at my feet, I stand
at the end of a shingle beach,
breaks in the mist playing
with a timid wind.

I am here for the ancient lore,
the talk, the songs,
the faces in the villages,
distantly familiar –
a grandmother's nightly tale
told before I slept.

I come to breathe
the country –
the shaggy mountain,
the river bend,
the meadow
where she began.

I taste blueberries
stolen from the heath
and feel a pale-eyed sun
trying to ripen them before
summer dies in the freeze of
northern winds.

The myths are here,
the leaning gravestones,
the crumbled towers and there,
beyond the water's edge, a swan,
not black but a foggy white,
glides like a silent wraith.

Scarf wrapped thick, hands
deep in gloves, I hear
the beat of oarlocks roll
from a fisherman's boat, a rhythm
matched by his craggy tune
and the plash of the waves he makes.

Inside my tourist skin, I learn how
the lakes, the rivers, the rocks back home
hold me
in the iron-silk bonds of memory.

Too late to tell her –
I know now
why Nanna wept.

Touching Down

I have wept at Gallipoli, held a candle,
pulled tight my coat.
I have touched a ghost gum in Santorini,
smelled the crushed leaf.

There were echoes at Epidaurus,
whisperings,
an ancient muse seeking entry to my soul
but I could not wait.

Now, I fly over my country,
the home harbour mapped in orange light.

Will you be here to meet me?
Will you forgive the words that I regret?

I long for my return to pink-seeded grasses
drooping on the edge of rain
guttering in furrows,
a return to strings of slow black cows,
legs spindled thin in mist.

My hands already know where
green chaff bales lie wrapped,
like enormous plastic eggs.

There used to be a speckled gecko
on the fly-wire door, a white-headed dove
nesting in the turpentines.
Will you say they came again this year?

I need to see the edgy sun-lines burned
early into frost around the ironbarks,
the carvings on river rocks.

I need to hear the thud of tennis balls
on loam, behind the church,
wind sighing through the nets.

After we touch down, I will search faces
in the great hall. Will I find you there?

The shuffle in the aisle is slow,
the hostess babbles her farewell patter.
I take first steps. I look for keys.

Incident at the Gallery

In the dark I watch a video.
The artist   eyes aglitter
expounds the skill of art's expression
the flight into sublimity
through unerring faith
that he is the light that paints
a universe within the room.

I leave his fervent eloquence
wander from the small dark space
ponder passion's connotations.
Should I test his arguments,
make a list, dash off a note
but hey –
my bag   where did I leave my bag?

I turn to blazing glare
frightened guides in my path
the area roped against me.

Through the door   I see it
bulging full of keys and pens
under peanut-butter sandwiches.
There it leans   slumped against
the cushioned seat.

Do not be afraid, I say, *that's mine,*
as I dash beneath forbidding arms.

Snorts threats curses
loudhailer reverberations assail
as I retrieve the misjudged little thing –
I tip suspect contents on the floor.

*Perhaps you could not know
that I would never harbour
such terrible intent.*

Too late for explanation
a strange commotion
bursts through the sculptured doors
thumps along the polished stone.

Here comes a marching
heavy-booted bomb squad
plus a fearless robot
beeping electric signals
of imperious determination
to save us all   save everything
but not itself   or my bag –
from the perils of a shaky
                    shaky world.

I let the guides explain.

Keys

I know his ways, his thoughts –
in fact he fills my time but
not all is as I want with him.

Whoever attains perfection?

Yet he has gathered me in
with his gentle talk,
his offer to help.

I am not the key to his existence,
nor is he to mine.
We walk together through ordinary doors
into ordinary days, at ease.

We discuss his ideas, attend to mine,
treat each as brilliant
and if they are not, make them so for us.
We are extraordinarily in tune
when we meet,
if we meet
even for the shortest time
there is almost perfection.

Our keys are not kept under mats.

As You Pass Me in the Hall

If I play out each day with you,
it is the mere flow of habit;
if I speak niceties with you,
the words are shadows and shields
of what hides beneath
this seeming composure.

Because I must lie to you every day
to be the angel you think I am,
oiling my feathers to smoothness
to fool your perception of me,
I take wing on the roiling of storms
to escape the politeness of you.

My hidden talons could pierce you,
could pin you bleeding to the wall.
I have a tongue that could shred
more readily than thunder bolts;
my black-centred ogre eye
could topple your terrible calm.

We are too wise for battle,
too aware of memory's bind;

once you were my gypsy love –
the golden earring, the laughing lips,
the heart full of songs for me.

We could crack the marble exteriors,
swing on dusty chandeliers,
lock up the house, billet the dog
and fly off to anywhere.

Turn your head, look at me.
Make your eyes say
there is a way through this.

Flat Sea

The beach is a rainbow of sometime surfers –
nothing to do but slow slow-talk,
order iced coffee in soft wax cups,
make hollows in the sand –
the rescue craft at water's edge,
a token in a flat, warm sea.

Becalmed, the young on aimless boards,
steer with lazy paddles.
The radio crackles in the lifeguard's hut,
'Storms forecast for late afternoon.'
Yellow flags begin to breathe –
the sea's skin ripples a mini-rise.

Beneath umbrellas bodies twitch,
like periscopes they raise their heads.
Children forgetting green Icy Poles,
squeal down to the sea with boogie boards;
Gran slips off her red-rubied scuffs
and the hoards troop down to the surf.

You bring coffee, cool, with froth,
a cup of pink ice cream with nuts.
We slap on sun lotion but sit in the shade,
small talk as lovers do.

We look beyond the march of waves,
smell salt in the rising breeze,
search the horizon for whale spouts out there,
out there in the wakening sea.

The storm, too distant to bother us yet,
we'll watch rumble in with interest;
until the lightning flickers too close
we'll sit and laugh at our daring.

I'll sip coffee, you'll spoon ice cream
and when the hail begins to sting,
we'll join the crowds and run.

We'll think about whales tomorrow.

The Lookout

The last time we were here,
we knew;
while gazing down into the valley,
while we searched for our place
in the distance,
while we recognised
the white-draped patch of vineyard,
and traced the blue-bright river
looping back and round itself,
we knew.

While we focussed binoculars on Jenny's house,
its training track a white ribbon,
we discovered dots of traffic
moving like toys on the highway,
caught the glint of red town-roofs,
bright clusters where the trees thinned
and noted the way the sun shone down
on clouds below us
to cast its own dark shadows.

When the absence of clarity at earth's edge,
the softly blurred horizon, invited thoughts of
floating down on giant wings,
the silent sway a weightless forgetting,
when our grown children, laughed, entertained,
photographed us,
we knew.

That was why everyone was here
but there – we all must own a final day,
some gently, some with pain,
some without warning
but oh, how I wished it wasn't
to be you;
you, behaving as if it were nothing
and we kept from despair
because of it.

And now, in the sunshine, the cold wind keens,
sighs without tears through casuarinas,
not knowing what we remember,
what we forget,
sweeps across the mountain's face
and is gone.

A Small Delight

My latest year was truly filled with macro events –
a wandering thing ate my orchid's stem of promise,
each eager bud methodically removed.

My ancient stove door crashed off its weary hinges,
cracked six floor tiles now obsolete –
and you, dear man, fixed both disasters.

In the afternoons, we strolled around the busy park,
dodged cricketers and their cheers, stray calves and wombat
markers claiming pathway edges.

Wild ducks jabbered on the pond, flocked to the other shore,
elbow-legged waterhens skulking in the skimpy reeds,
pretended invisibility.

We talked about this and everything inside our thought lines,
your unnerving diagnosis reversed, my fearful apprehension
of finite change on hold.

More years now possible, now believable,
we settled then for unexpected time, for technicolour dawns
flaring any and every weather.

We didn't ask for reasons. There was only one clear certainty,
that we were there, in that joyful moment with our small delight –
tomorrow's beckoning.

The Eye Beholding

It's too much,
an ibis arrowing,
a peacock feathering –
too much
a silky web against my cheek,
the chiffon air.

I am benumbed –
so many things to choose from.
I wait and watch, hatch the words
to wrap them in with
footnotes
on every variation.

It's just too much –
clouds roll over the mountain crest
spill into the valley fold
a mantle,
against the orange cliff,
a misted breath, so different from
summer's choking blast.
Exploded canopies, blackened trunks
give way
to eager red-flushed growth.
The trees along the creek show off
their short-cropped heads.

And here
in the grass, a lilac lily fringes,
a dead leaf cha-chas on the patio,
then
a yellow-wattled streak breaks through the view,
snatches soft spiders from under the eaves,
as if plucking grapes.

It's all too much,
this promise –
yet not enough;
the eye beholding falters,
unable,
until
a new day pulses
morning's proof again.

www.ingramcontent.com/pod-product-compliance
Lightning Source LLC
Chambersburg PA
CBHW062156100526
44589CB00014B/1855